Stop Reading, Start Studying:
Inductive Bible Study Method Explained

Henry Jackson III

Ordering Information:

Quantity sales. Special discounts are available on quantity purchases by non-profits, ministries, churches, corporations, associations, and others. For details, contact the publisher via email at sales@inductivebiblestudyapp.com.

Printed in the United States of America

First Printing, 2016

ISBN
Paperback: 978-0-9970743-4-5
Kindle: 978-0-9970743-6-9

www.InductiveBibleStudyApp.com

Because of the dynamic nature of the internet, any web addresses or links contained in this book may have changed since publication and may no longer be valid.

All Scripture quotations, unless otherwise noted, are taken from:

At Inductive Bible Study LLC, our mission is simple – "make disciples of all nations" (Matt. 28:19). We are committed to providing high quality tools, resources, and training to assist Christ's church in fulfilling the Great Commission.

Thank you for purchasing or downloading one of our resources!

Also available:

Book

The premier book on how to enrich your study of God's word using the Inductive Bible Study method!

Paperback: 978-0- 9970743-0- 7

Kindle: 978-0- 9970743-1- 4

ePub: 978-0- 9970743-2- 1

Audiobook: 978-0- 9970743-3- 8

Student Workbook

This five lesson study provides practical steps on how to study the Bible inductively, memorize & meditate on Scripture, and pray effectively.

Paperback: 978-0- 9970743-5- 2

Leader Guide

This guide empowers small group leaders with discussion starters, background commentary and easy to follow lesson plans.

Paperback: 978-0- 9970743-4- 5

Kindle: 978-0- 9970743-6- 9

If this resource has helped you enhance in your walk with God, please help spread the word about us.

Facebook: /InductiveBibleStudyApp

Twitter: @iBibleStudyApp

Google+: InductiveBibleStudyApp

Email: info@ibible.study

YouTube: InductiveBibleStudyApp

Web: http://ibible.study

Check out our free IBS app - http://InductiveBibleStudyApp.com

Table of Contents

Introduction

Welcome to Inductive Bible Study!

If you have never studied the Bible before, or if you have been a follower of Jesus for some time but desire to understand more of the "deep and hidden things" God promises He will reveal for those who read and study His Word (Dan. 2:22), this book is for you. By following a few simple steps, and committing to learn the *how* of Inductive Bible Study, you will come to a more intimate relationship with God. In addition, by using this easy-to-follow guide you will learn how to accurately interpret and apply God's Word, thereby experiencing its life transforming power!

The first three lessons of the book will walk you through the steps to Inductive Bible Study. Then, lesson 4 will talk about the importance of memorizing and meditating on Scripture. Lesson 5 emphasizes the integral role that prayer plays in Bible study. Finally, you'll find the workbook fill-in, which provides answers for all of the blanks found in the book – but no peeking! An overview of the Inductive Bible Study app is provided in the appendix followed by a copy of the helpful charts presented in the workbook. Feel free to make as many copies of the charts as you'd like.

Lesson 1

OBSERVATION: WHAT DOES IT SAY?

Learn the importance of paying close attention to the words of Scripture while also practicing strategies for identifying and marking key words.

Lesson 2

INTERPRETATION: WHAT DOES IT MEAN?

Explore the principles of sound biblical interpretation and survey several the external resources that will prove invaluable in the interpretive process.

Lesson 3

APPLICATION: HOW DO I RESPOND?

Consider the ramifications of understanding yet ignoring the commands of Scripture and also discover practical ways to create biblically based goals.

Lesson 4

MEMORIZATION & MEDITATION: THY WORD IS IN MY HEART

Reflect upon the importance of saturating our hearts and minds with the Word of God and suggest tools and techniques which will help build Biblical memory.

Lesson 5

PRAYER: TALKING TO GOD

Provide a working definition of prayer and outline how essential prayer is to an enriching Bible study experience.

This workbook serves as a great companion to the associated book (*Stop Reading, Start Studying: Inductive Bible Study Method Explained*), but will also function independently as it contains lots of additional information, charts, and activities. Millions have been blessed by the Inductive Bible Study method and it is our prayer that you, your church, or your ministry will be blessed by it as well!

This is a great curriculum for Bible study workshops, vacation Bible schools, and conferences. Each lesson lends itself to the flexibility of being completed in one setting or it can be broken up into multiple sessions. If you are planning on leading a group through this curriculum, we suggest you purchase the Leader Guide and have students walk through the Student Guide. The Leader Guide offers awesome illustrations / discussion starters and commentary that will help new teachers feel absolutely comfortable teaching this course, while also going in-depth on various topics for the advanced teacher.

Inductive Bible Study is not hard! But it does take time and a desire to learn. The techniques laid out in the *Stop Reading, Start Studying: Inductive Bible Study Method Explained* Workbook will change the way you read, study and interpret the Bible, and ultimately, they will change your life.

You will never be the same again. You will be *transformed.*

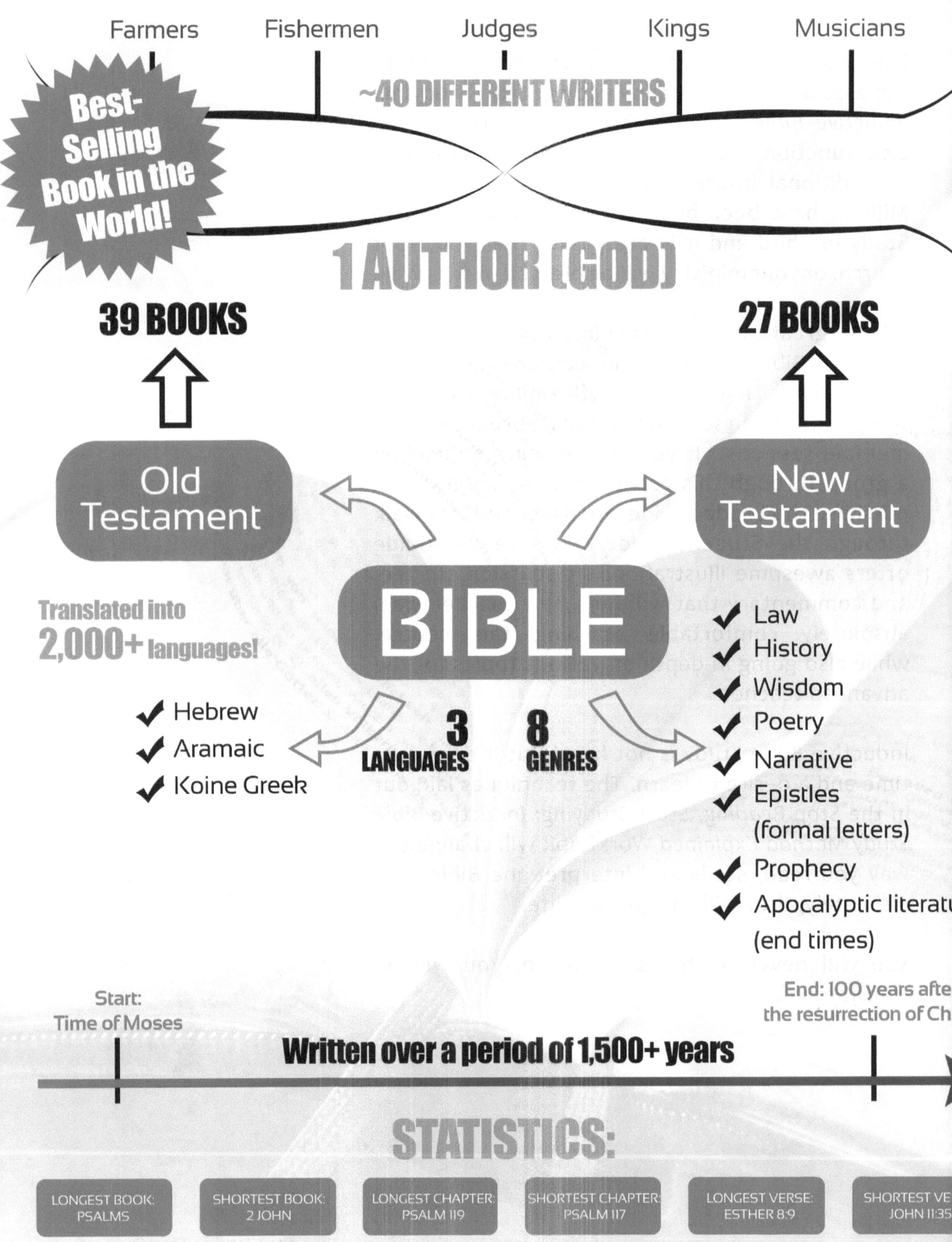

Farmers
Fishermen
Judges
Kings
Musicians
~40 DIFFERENT WRITERS
Best-Selling Book in the World!
1 AUTHOR (GOD)
39 BOOKS
27 BOOKS
Old Testament
New Testament
BIBLE
Translated into 2,000+ languages!
Hebrew
Aramaic
Koine Greek
3 LANGUAGES
8 GENRES
Law
History
Wisdom
Poetry
Narrative
Epistles (formal letters)
Prophecy
Apocalyptic literature (end times)
Start: Time of Moses
End: 100 years after the resurrection of Ch
Written over a period of 1,500+ years
STATISTICS:
LONGEST BOOK: PSALMS
SHORTEST BOOK: 2 JOHN
LONGEST CHAPTER: PSALM 119
SHORTEST CHAPTER: PSALM 117
LONGEST VERSE: ESTHER 8:9
SHORTEST VE JOHN 11:35

LESSON 1

Observation: What Does It Say?

> "The goal of observation is to enable one to become saturated with the particulars of a passage so that one is thoroughly conscious of the object being observed."
>
> – Robert Traina

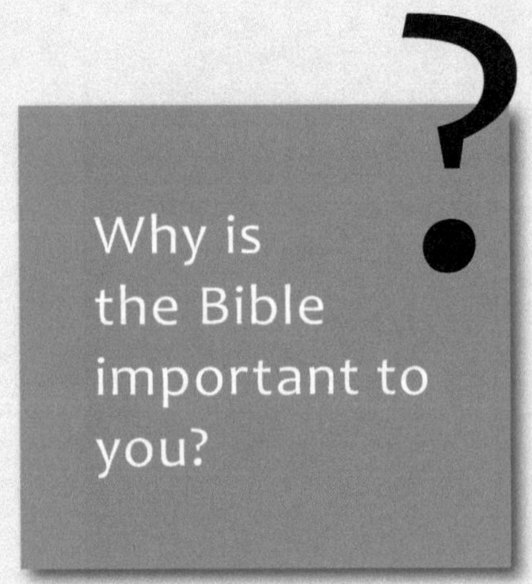

Key Verse

"All Scripture is
inspired by God
and profitable for
teaching, for reproof,
for correction,
for training in
righteousness; so
that the man of God
may be adequate,
equipped for every
good work."
– 2 Timothy 3:16–17

Discussion Starter

In January 1984, I was painting the home of an 89-year-old lady in Spokane. She had a large family Bible prominently displayed on the coffee table and remarked that it was 116 years old and a priceless heirloom. I commented on how remarkable that was, and added, "It doesn't matter how old the Bible might be, what's on the inside is what matters." She immediately replied, "Oh, I know. That sure is the truth. Why, we have family records and births and marriages and deaths that go so far back, all recorded in that Bible; we could never replace them." – John Underhill

Objective

To learn the importance of paying close attention to the words of Scripture while also practicing strategies for identifying and marking key words.

Lesson

The Power of God's Word

The Bible is unlike anything you will ever read, and it provides wisdom you will never find in any book.

 It is unique in its:

a. *Authorship* – This is the only book in history that contains the direct revelation of God.

"But know this first of all, that no prophecy of Scripture is a matter of one's own interpretation, for no prophecy was ever made by an act of human will, but men moved by the Holy Spirit spoke from God."
– 2 Peter 1:20–21

b. *Authority* – As the creator, owner, and sustainer of everything, its author speaks with supreme force.

"So will My word be which goes forth from My mouth; It will not return to Me empty, Without accomplishing what I desire, And without succeeding in the matter for which I sent it."
– Isaiah 55:11

c. *Accuracy* – While mankind speculates, the Bible speaks truth.

"Sanctify them in the truth; Your word is truth."
– John 17:1

d. *Adequacy* – Today's best-selling self-help books will soon become irrelevant, but God's Word stands the test of time!

"You, however, continue in the things you have learned and become convinced of, knowing from whom you have learned them, and that from childhood you have known the sacred writings which are able to give you the wisdom that leads to salvation through faith which is in Christ Jesus."
– 2 Timothy 3:14–15

e. *Agenda* – How many other books outline the path to obtaining eternal life? None!

"These things I have written to you who believe in the name of the Son of God, so that you may know that you have eternal life."
– 1 John 5:13

"Therefore many other signs Jesus also performed in the presence of the disciples, which are not written in this book; but these have been written so that you may believe that Jesus is the Christ, the Son of God; and that believing you may have life in His name."
– John 20:30–31

2 The Holy Spirit has anointed every word in the Bible and it has the power to *transform* you. But, you must be willing to engage and *wrestle* with those words for transformation to happen!

What is Observation?

The first and most important step in Inductive Bible Study is *observation*. Observation describes "the act of taking notice, fixing the mind upon, and beholding with attention, with the goal of discovering what the text says."[1]

1 Observation attempts to *discover* what the passage says.

Observation involves examining the obvious. Dr. H. T. Kuist defines observation as, "the art of seeing things as they really are." Facts about people, places and events are pretty easy to distinguish in biblical writing because the writers tend to repeat these facts. Let the text speak for itself. Don't try to read anything into a passage of Scripture, or attempt to "spiritualize" it.

2 Your main goal for this first step is to try and establish the author's *original intent*.

"How many books have you ever read where you had the benefit of the author's presence to help you discern his original intent?" – Anonymous

3 Establish *context*.

Establishing context will lay the foundation for accurate interpretation. Context means, "That which goes with the text." It is the setting in which a passage occurs. Thus, it's important to

1

» Always start with prayer. The Bible tells us there are wonderful mysteries waiting for us when we study Scripture: "... that [you] may behold Wonderful things from [His] law" (Ps. 119:18).

» More on prayer will be covered in Lesson 5.

2

» What was the author trying to communicate to his readers?

» Students must be careful not to presuppose they already know the author's original intent based on their familiarity with the passage.

---

1   "Inductive Bible Study: Observation." *Inductive Bible Study: Observation.* N.p., n.d. Web. 24 Oct. 2015.
< http://www.preceptaustin.org/observation.htm>.

examine those verses immediately before and after the passage you are studying. Consider also the book in which the passage appears, as well as other books by the same author. Doing so will help determine how the passage fits into the overall message of the entire Bible.

"From the standpoint of the Bible as literature, the simplest error of reading is the failure to consider the immediate context of the verse or passage in question. The literature of the cults is filled with illustrations of this basic mistake."[2] – James Sire, Scripture Twisting: 20 Ways the Cults Misread the Bible

4 Look for obvious things—*people*, *places*, and *events* that are usually easy to identify.

In the epistles (such as Galatians, 1 & 2 Corinthians or 1 & 2 Timothy), start by observing facts about the author and the letter's recipients. By starting with the obvious, things within a book that are not as easy to see or understand or are confusing will eventually become clearer.

5 Research relevant *background* information.

Consider also the cultural setting of the text. The Bible was originally written within many different cultural backgrounds, which will affect how you understand the passage. For example, Paul asked the question in 1 Corinthians 11:13: "Is it proper for a woman to pray to God with her

______

2   Sire, James W. *Scripture Twisting: 20 Ways the Cults Misread the Bible*. Downers Grove, IL: InterVarsity, 1980. Print.

5

» If you don't quite know where to turn to research various topics, we'll cover that in Lesson 2 – Interpretation.

» Quick research will reveal that in ancient Judaism, women covered their heads not only for prayer but whenever they were outside of their homes. Knowing this simple fact will help when trying to figure out later on why Paul was asking this question!

head uncovered?" See if you can find out why this was important in ancient Jewish culture.

Contemplate, too, the genre of the book you are studying. The Bible contains poetry, wise sayings, history, letters (epistles), prophetic writings, and apocalyptic (prophetic) literature. Understanding genre will affect how you later interpret a passage.

6 One of the most helpful ways to perform observation is by identifying and marking _key words_.

Typically, key words are repeated words that are key to one paragraph but sometimes the entire chapter or book. You will complete this step by marking these words or phrases in your Bible by placing a symbol or color over the key word or phrase, to identify it quickly.

a. Read 1 Corinthians 13:1–4 and see if you can identify the key word.

"If I speak with the tongues of men and of angels, but do not have love, I have become a noisy gong or a clanging cymbal. If I have the gift of prophecy, and know all mysteries and all knowledge; and if I have all faith, so as to remove mountains, but do not have love, I am nothing. And if I give all my possessions to feed the poor, and if I surrender my body to be burned, but do not have love, it profits me nothing. Love is patient, love is kind and is not jealous; love does not brag and is not arrogant..."

6
» Marking the keyword "love" helps students focus on the main point of the passage. Otherwise, it would be easy to veer off course and focus on speaking with tongues, the gift of prophecy, or faith that moves mountains. In this passage, these are merely used to show that without love, the greatest of gifts are profitless.

b. Which word did you see repeated several times? *Love*

c. Now, go back and mark the key word "love" with a heart - ♥

d. How do you think marking keywords will enhance your study of the Bible?

____

____

____

____

____

7 Like an investigative reporter who interrogates by asking formal and methodical questions, train yourself to examine the text. In Inductive Bible Study, we do this by asking the "*Big 6*" Questions.

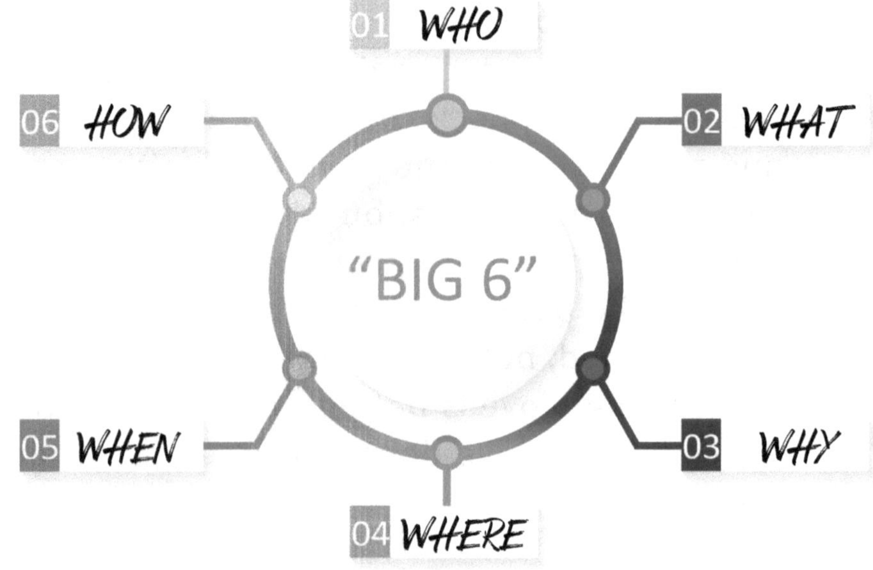

7

» For example: Who is speaking? What is the author doing? Why was this book written? Where did something happen? When was the book or passage written? How will (or did) something happen?

» You will start to acquire insights into the Word of God that you could not have discovered from a quick surface reading, and you will begin to experience the joy of self-discovery.

Don't be frustrated if you are not able to answer every one of the "Big 6" Questions every time; this is ok and common. Asking these questions will force you to slow down and counteract the tendency to read through a passage hastily. Doing so will help you avoid presumptions and fallacies that lead to false teaching. As we've said, the Word of God speaks for itself.

8 Identify a *central theme*.

The theme will tend to center on a main person, event, teaching or subject; it will often be revealed in your list of key words, and by an additional reading of the text. Hopefully, the theme is obvious. Ask yourself: *What seems to be the central focus of the book or the chapter of the book?*

"Whenever a person begins to approach a book, a chapter or a section, the central theme or subject must be grasped and this comes only by reading it over and over again until the central theme stands out as the sun illuminating the rest of the material."
– Pastor Xavior Reis, *Calvary Chapel Pasadena*

9 Look for *connecting* words and phrases.

Connecting words and phrases join clauses, passages, paragraphs, and chapters together. Though they may seem insignificant, they are powerful words that connect the writer's train of thought into a unified whole.

8

» In general, you will want to make it a practice to state the central theme of a chapter or a group of verses in an accurate, concise, manner.

a. Terms of *Conclusion*

A term of conclusion identifies a logical consequence or conclusion or summarizes a preceding argument. Terms of conclusion are words and phrases like *Therefore, So, For this reason,* and *So then.*

Underline the term of conclusion in Matthew 12:12:

"How much more valuable then is a man than a sheep! **So then**, it is lawful to do good on the Sabbath."

b. Terms of *Explanation*

Terms of explanation introduce the reason for something, making it plain or understandable. These words give reasons why something is true or why something occurred, or give additional information. Sometimes they express cause or give additional information. Terms of conclusion are words like *For* and *Because.*

Underline the term of explanation in Romans 1:16:

"**For** I am not ashamed of the gospel, **for** it is the power of God for salvation to everyone who believes, to the Jew first and also to the Greek."

c. Terms of *Purpose*

Terms of purpose indicate the intended or end goal of an idea or action, or the effect, aim, design or consequence of something. They provide the reason something is done. Terms of purpose are words or phrases such as *So that, In order that* (or *In order to*) and *That.*

Underline the terms of purpose in Exodus 20:20:

"Do not be afraid; for God has come **in order to** test you, and **in order that** the fear of Him may remain with you, **so that** you may not sin."

d. Terms of *Contrast*

Terms of contrast distinguish between two opposing terms or phrases. They will usually be evident by the words or phrases *But, But rather, However, In spite of, Instead of, Nevertheless, On the other hand,* and *Yet.*

Underline the term of contrast in Romans 6:23.

"For the wages of sin is death, **but** the free gift of God is eternal life in Christ Jesus our Lord."

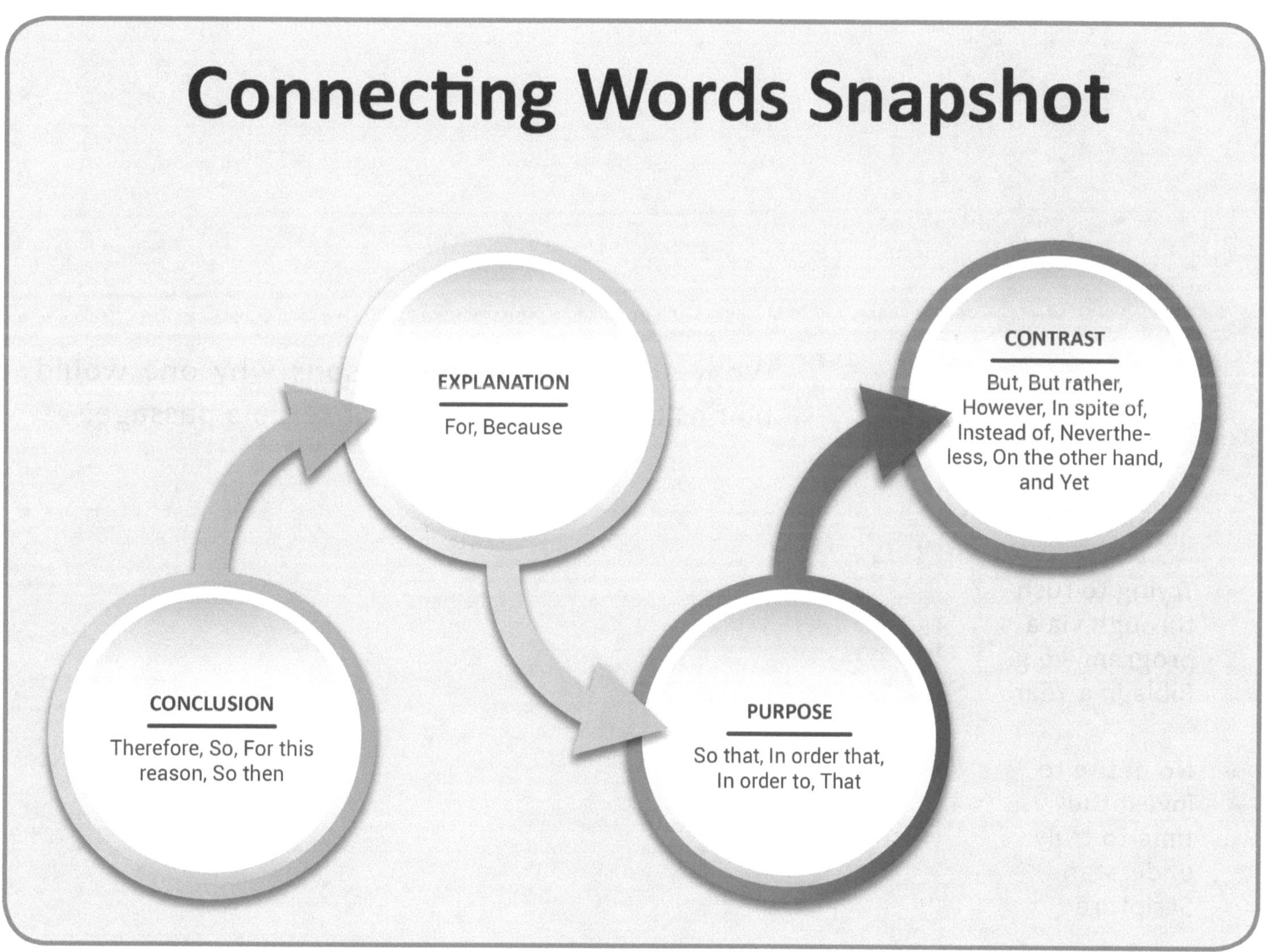

Discussion

1 What are some of the dangers of not adequately observing the Scriptures?

1
» Adding things that are not there – e.g. "apple" in the Garden

» Missing things that are important

____

____

____

____

____

____

2 What are some of the reasons why one would be hesitant to thoroughly observe a passage?

2
» Lack of time

» Trying to rush through via a program – e.g. Bible in a Year

» No desire to invest the time to truly understand Scripture

____

____

____

____

____

____

3 What do you believe you will gain by taking the time to observe verses in the Bible?

____

____

____

____

____

____

4 Discuss a time when you sent someone a text or email asking them to do something and they did the wrong thing because they skimmed over it.

____

____

____

____

____

3

» Deeper understanding of Scripture

» Increased ability to identify the central theme or point of a passage.

4

» Responses will vary.

» Be prepared to offer an example of your own.

5 Do you think God wants us to pay attention to the details of His Word? How do you think He feels when we skim over His Word as we do online articles?

____

____

____

____

____

____

6 Cult leaders thrive on followers who don't examine the Scriptures for themselves. What is the correlation between the formation of cults and the lack of observing the Scriptures in their proper context?

____

____

____

____

____

Jonestown Massacre

Source: http://www.history.com/topics/jonestown

On November 18, 1978, in what became known as the "Jonestown Massacre," more than 900 members of an American cult called the Peoples Temple died in a mass suicide-murder under the direction of their leader Jim Jones (1931-78). The mass suicide-murder took place at the so-called Jonestown settlement in the South American nation of Guyana. Jones had founded what became the Peoples Temple in Indiana in the 1950s then relocated his congregation to California in the 1960s. In the 1970s, following negative media attention, the powerful, controlling preacher moved with some 1,000 of his followers to the Guyanese jungle, where he promised they would establish a utopian community. On November 18, 1978, U.S. Representative Leo Ryan, who had gone to Jonestown to investigate claims of abuse, was murdered, along with four members of his delegation, by Jonestown gunmen. That same day, Jones ordered his followers to ingest poison-laced punch, while armed guards stood by.

> *How beneficial would it have been for the members of Peoples Temple to observe the text? Do you think they would have found a passage that supported suicide?*

"For the time will come when they will not endure sound doctrine; but wanting to have their ears tickled, they will accumulate for themselves teachers in accordance to their own desires, and will turn away their ears from the truth and will turn aside to myths."
- 2 Timothy 4:3–4

Activity

Let's get used to identifying the Big 6 Questions (*Who, What, Why, When, Where and How?*), marking key words that repeat (with a symbol) and connecting words (*Therefore, So, For this reason, So then, For, Because, So that, In order that, That*). For each verse listed, see if you can mark the keywords with the suggested marking, and fill in the blanks below the verse.

 Read John 1:1–4

"In the beginning was the Word, and the Word was with God, and the Word was God. He was in the beginning with God. All things came into being through Him, and apart from Him nothing came into being that has come into being. In Him was life, and the life was the Light of men."

Apply the Following Marking	
Word(s)	Symbol
God, Word, He, or Him	✝

Answer the following "Big 6" Questions	
Who is the main person of this passage?	*The Word, God*
What has this person done?	*Brought all things into being; Giver of life; Light of men*
How long has this person been in existence?	*Since the beginning*

The "Big 6" Questions are not meant to help you interpret the meaning of the text, but simply to observe what the text says. The answers for your questions should come directly from the text. You should quote the text as much as possible when responding.

Leader Insight

 Read Exodus 20:20

"Do not be afraid; for God has come in order to test you, and in order that the fear of Him may remain with you, so that you may not sin."

Apply the Following Marking	
Word(s)	Symbol
afraid, fear	

Answer the following Big "6" Questions	
Who should I fear?	God
What is the command of this verse?	Do not be afraid
What has happened that would cause those involved to be afraid?	God has come
Why is this command given?	In order that the fear of God may remain in you So that you may not sin.
Why has God come?	In order to test them.

Leader Insight

Students can ask the same Big 6 Questions in different ways. See the different versions of "What" and "Why" questions above.

<table>
<tr><td colspan="3">Identify the Connecting Words</td></tr>
<tr><td>Type</td><td>Word</td><td>Connected Thoughts</td></tr>
<tr><td>Conclusion</td><td>So</td><td>Fear God…So that you may not sin.</td></tr>
<tr><td>Explanation</td><td>For</td><td>Don't be afraid…for God has come</td></tr>
<tr><td>Purpose</td><td>In order to</td><td>God has come…in order to test you</td></tr>
</table>

3 Read Philippians 2:12–13

"So then, my beloved, just as you have always obeyed, not as in my presence only, but now much more in my absence, work out your salvation with fear and trembling; for it is God who is at work in you, both to will and to work for His good pleasure."

Apply the Following Marking	
Word(s)	Symbol
Work	

Answer the following Big "6" Questions	
Who is to work?	*My beloved*
What are they commanded to do?	*Work out their salvation*
How are they to work?	*With fear and trembling*
Who will help them?	*God is at work in them*
What is the goal of their Helper?	*Both to will and to work His good pleasure*

Type	Word	Connected Thoughts
Conclusion	So then	So then...work out your salvation
Explanation	For	Work out your salvation...for it is God who is at work in you
Contrast	But	You have always obeyed in my presence...but now much more in my absence

LESSON *2*

Interpretation: What Does It Mean?

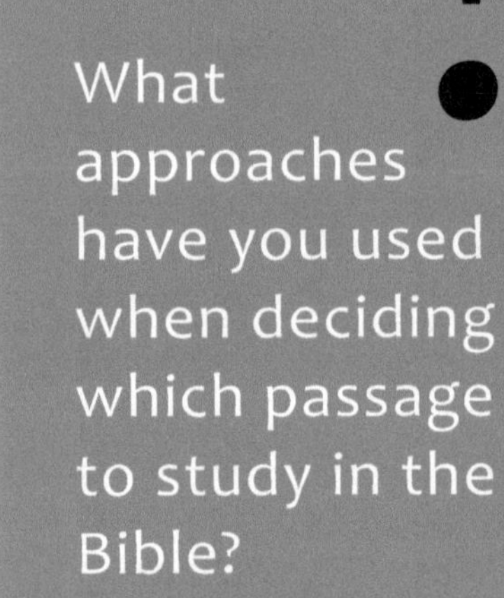

What approaches have you used when deciding which passage to study in the Bible?

Key Verse

"And beginning with Moses and all the Prophets, He interpreted to them in all the Scriptures the things concerning Himself."

– Luke 24:27 (ESV)

Discussion Starter

When the preacher's car broke down on a country road, he walked to a nearby roadhouse to use the phone. After calling for a tow truck, he spotted his old friend, Frank, drunk and shabbily dressed at the bar. "What happened to you, Frank?" asked the good reverend. "You used to be rich."

Frank told a sad tale of bad investments that had led to his downfall. "Go home," the preacher said. "Open your Bible at random, stick your finger on the page and there will be God's answer."

Some time later, the preacher bumped into Frank, who was wearing a Gucci suit, sporting a Rolex watch and had just stepped out of a Mercedes. "Frank." said the preacher, "I am glad to see things really turned around for you."

"Yes, preacher, and I owe it all to you," said Frank. "I opened my Bible, put my finger down on the page and there was the answer—Chapter 11."

Key Verse Commentary

In the final chapter of Luke's Gospel, we read of two disciples of Jesus who were walking from Jerusalem to Emmaus on the day that Jesus rose from the dead. As they traveled, a man joined them—the resurrected Jesus—although they did not recognize Him. As they walked, Jesus interpreted the Old Testament to them. How wonderful it must have been to have the author of the Bible to explain its meaning to them? You can have the same experience today, for we have been given the Holy Spirit to serve as our greatest teacher!

Objective

To explore the principles of sound biblical interpretation and survey several external resources that will prove invaluable in the interpretive process.

Lesson

Rightly Divide the Word of Truth

The Bible is a Divine book that contains the revelation of God's plan of redemption over all time. It is a book of mystery, intrigue, comfort, sorrow, encouragement and great joy. Above all, it communicates the heart of God.

Peter exhorts followers of Jesus to strive to "rightly [divide] the word of truth" in 2 Timothy 2:15 (KJV). Interpreting Scripture must be done correctly and with reverence.

What is Interpretation?

Dr. Howard Hendricks compared interpretation to a building: "In observation we excavate. In interpretation we erect." A building's stability is determined by its foundation. The more secure the foundation, the more dependable the structure. In the same way, interpretation will come more readily and be more secure when the observation process has been thoroughly completed.

1 Webster's Dictionary defines interpretation as explaining or telling the meaning of something and presenting it in _understandable terms_.

(2) Biblical interpretation, also called hermeneutics, seeks to walk in the _author's shoes_ with the ultimate goal being able to understand or explain their original intent.

"But know this first of all, that no prophecy of Scripture is a matter of one's own interpretation, for no prophecy was ever made by an act of human will, but men _moved by the Holy Spirit_ spoke from God."
– 2 Peter 1:20–21

General Principles of Interpretation

Sometimes it will be tempting to try and force the Scriptures to agree with whatever you want the passage to say; this is a misleading and risky trap. Misinterpretation is far too common among students of the Bible. How can this be avoided? Applying the following simple interpretive principles will help you guard against interpreting the Bible incorrectly.

(1) Base your interpretation on the author's _original intent_.

Many times people will base interpretation on popular accord, gut feelings, powerful or persuasive arguments, or even what other respected teachers and scholars have taught. However, interpretation must be based on the author's intended meaning, not the reader's opinion or anyone else's. The context the author wrote in, as well as the history, grammar, culture,

(1)

» It has been some 2000 years since many of those authors documented God's Word, and their world was very different than ours!

» One of the great leaders of the Reformation in Switzerland, Ulrich Zwingli says interpreting without considering what the author intended is like "breaking off a flower from its roots."

literary form, and conventions the author was working in must be considered.

To understand the importance of context in interpretation, consider the sentence, "It was a ball." What exactly does this phrase mean?

The answer depends on the context! Consider the following:

A The baseball umpire saw the pitch drift to the outside and said, *It was a ball.*

B We went to the dance last night; it was so formal, *it was a ball.*

C As I was walking along the golf course, I spotted something small and white in the tall grass. *It was a ball.*

D I had so much fun at the game night. *It was a ball.*

In each sentence above, "ball" means something different. Context is necessary to determine the true meaning. Try to guard against interpreting a text in isolation from the context it was written in. You will find it helpful when interpreting Scripture to give the most weight to the nearest context.

2 Read and interpret the Bible *literally*, when it makes good sense.

In addition to interpreting Scripture based on the author's original intent, hold to the normal literal meaning of the text. Constantly searching for some deeper spiritual meaning is guaranteed to take you off-track. There are of course spiritual aspects to many passages; however, the authors normally make this clear.

» Some questions to consider when discovering the cultural and historical context:

- What were the times like when this passage was written?

- What was the attitude toward Christianity when this was written?

- When was this passage taking place?

- What were some of the social and political influences on the writer and on those to whom he was writing?

The best argument for taking the Bible literally is because Jesus Himself did. When the Scribes and Pharisees demanded Jesus perform a sign to prove who He said he was, Jesus referred to a familiar text in the Hebrew Scriptures that those Scribes and Pharisees knew well:

"An evil and adulterous generation craves for a sign; and yet no sign will be given to it but the sign of Jonah the prophet; for just as Jonah was three days and three nights in the belly of the sea monster, so will the Son of Man be three days and three nights in the heart of the earth." – Matthew 12:39–40

Did Jesus refer to the example of Jonah as if it were a literal event? ☐ Yes ☐ No

Jesus interpreted the Scriptures literally and so should we!

"If the literal meaning of any word or expression makes good sense in its connections, it is literal; but if the literal meaning does not make good sense, it is figurative. Since the literal is the most usual signification of a word, and, therefore, occurs much more frequently than the figurative, any term should be regarded as literal until there is good reason for a different understanding." – Clinton Lockhart, *Principles of Interpretation*

Lord's Supper

"For I received from the Lord that which I also delivered to you, that the Lord Jesus in the night in which He was betrayed took bread; and when He had given thanks, He broke it and said, "This is My body, which is for you; do this in remembrance of Me." In the same way He took the cup also after supper, saying, "This cup is the new covenant in My blood; do this, as often as you drink it, in remembrance of Me."
– 1 Corinthians 11:23–25

Was the Lord's Supper an example of Jesus promoting cannibalism (eating flesh)?
☐ Yes ☐ No

3 Compare Scripture with *Scripture*.

This means interpretation of a passage should never be done in isolation to the rest of the Bible. At the very minimum, examine the paragraph in which the passage is embedded. Then read the passage within the context of the chapter, and then in light of the book as a whole. Cross-reference other passages that may shed light on the one you are studying.

Let's start with a very popular phrase that is often used to support seeking one's own revenge:

"...eye for eye, tooth for tooth, hand for hand, foot for foot..."
– Exodus 21:24

> "God spoke to us that we might know truth. Therefore, take the Word of God at face value—in its natural, normal sense. Look first for the clear teaching of Scripture, not a hidden meaning. Understand and recognize figures of speech and interpret them accordingly."
> – Kay Arthur, *How to Study Your Bible*

» Sometimes parallel passages in other Bible books can shed light on the meaning of a passage which is obscure in its immediate context.

» Scripture never contradicts itself.

» The Bible is its own best commentary.

» By comparing one verse with other verses, we can reach definite conclusions about what it does *not* teach, too!

Now let's take a step back and view this directive in a larger context:

"If men struggle with each other and strike a woman with child so that she gives birth prematurely, yet there is no injury, he shall surely be fined as the woman's husband may demand of him, and he shall pay as the judges decide. "But if there is any further injury, then you shall appoint as a penalty life for life, eye for eye, tooth for tooth, hand for hand, foot for foot, burn for burn, wound for wound, bruise for bruise."
– Exodus 21:22–25

Consider the context of the audience. The nation of Israel had recently been freed from 400 years of slavery (Genesis 15:13). At this point, they had no constitution or formal judicial system to abide by. God was in the process of transforming a group of rebellious ex-slaves into His holy people. In order to accomplish this, He laid out very specific laws regarding how they were to handle civil affairs.

Later, as Jesus delivers the Sermon on the Mount, we find Him elevating the importance of following the law of mercy beyond that of Israel's moral law.

"You have heard that it was said, 'AN EYE FOR AN EYE, AND A TOOTH FOR A TOOTH.' "But I say to you, do not resist an evil person; but whoever slaps you on your right cheek, turn the other to him also."
– Matthew 5:38–39

Turning the other cheek means not to return insult for insult in retaliation, which is quite typical of those who do not follow Christ. The laws of the Old Testament were designed to serve as a tutor that would ultimately lead us to Christ (Gal. 3:24). Jesus offers the perfect example of how to trust God's vengeance (Deut. 32:35) in the face of accusers, as He prayed for their forgiveness (Luke 23:34) while being crucified unjustly.

4 Seek *external* resources.

The first tool every student of the Bible should obtain is a good study Bible with notes that explain historical and cultural background information. These will prove invaluable in the interpretive process. Second, he or she should have access to a variety of evangelical commentaries. In this day, there are many wonderful commentaries that can be easily accessed on the Internet.

EXTERNAL RESOURCES

Tool	Purpose
Concordance	An alphabetical listing of biblical words that reference everywhere these words occur in specific translations of the Bible.
Expository Dictionary	Provide more holistic definitions, names and verse references for biblical words.
Biblical Encyclopedia	Contain articles and definitions for words and terms in the Bible and also include historical context and verse references.
Bible Atlas	Provide geographical, topographical, historical, archaeological, and cultural perspectives on the Bible.
Bible Lexicon	Provide definitions and meaning of Biblical words found in the original New Testament Greek and Old Testament Hebrew languages of the Holy Bible.

 Identify *figures of speech* and *parables* in their historical context.

Though we are to interpret Scripture from a literal perspective, the Bible is also full of metaphorical language, figures of speech and stories. When it is clear the author is using one of these literary techniques, interpret what appears to be metaphorical against historical data to see if the meaning was different in the time it was written.

Figures of speech such as similes, metaphors, hyperbole and personification increase the power of a word or the force of an expression.

Common Figures of Speech Found in the Bible		
Type	Meaning	Example
Simile	The comparison between two unlike things using the words "like" or "as."	"Husbands, love your wives, just as Christ also loved the church and gave Himself up for her." (Eph. 5:25)
Metaphor	The comparison of two unlike things or ideas.	"I am the vine, you are the branches; he who abides in Me and I in him, he bears much fruit, for apart from Me you can do nothing." (John 15:5)
Hyperbole	The use of exaggeration for emphasis for effect.	"Saul and Jonathan, beloved and pleasant in their life, And in their death they were not parted; They were swifter than eagles, They were stronger than lions." (2 Sam. 1:23)
Personification	Giving human qualities to non-living things or ideas.	"The eyes of the LORD are toward the righteous and His ears are open to their cry." (Ps. 34:15)

6 Identify _timeless_ principles.

You'll also want to look for clues to the timelessness of a given statement that might be expressing an enduring theological principle. God is the same God today that He was back when the Bible's authors penned their work. Sometimes Scripture defines God's responses to specific behavior going on in the past, but it may also reveal something about God's character that will never change.

"Jesus Christ is the same yesterday and today and forever."
– Hebrews 13:8

Leader Insight

For example, God continually reprimanded Israel for the nation's disobedience and worship of other gods. Eventually, God disciplined Israel by allowing other powerful nations like Assyria and Babylon to oppress and ultimately disperse the Jewish people. Do these examples apply to modern-day readers? Absolutely. God's message has always been to "have no other god's before me" (Ex. 20:3; Deut. 5:7). This command has never changed. We can do much to learn from the example of Israel's disobedience set out in Scripture.

5

» When it is clear the author is using one of these literary techniques, interpret what appears to be metaphorical against historical data to see if the meaning was different back when it was written.

» Don't settle for a figure of speech unless it is clearly indicated as such.

> By looking up other cross-references, you'll get a much bigger and clearer picture of what God has said in all of his Word, not just that one context.
> – Rick Warren

7 Compare multiple *translations.*

The Bible was originally written primarily in Greek and Hebrew. A small portion of the book of Daniel was written in Aramaic. The first person to translate the Bible into English from Latin was William Tyndale in the 16th Century. Today there are hundreds of different English versions of Bibles.

Consider the simple graphic below showing the difference in translations. The versions on the left are the most wooden, word-for-word translations. Moving right, the translations become more thought-for thought.

Proverbs 18:24	
KJV	A man that hath friends must shew himself friendly: and there is a friend that sticketh closer than a brother.
NASB	A man of too many friends comes to ruin, But there is a friend who sticks closer than a brother.
ESV	A man of many companions may come to ruin, but there is a friend who sticks closer than a brother.
NIV	One who has unreliable friends soon comes to ruin, but there is a friend who sticks closer than a brother.
NLT	There are "friends" who destroy each other, but a real friend sticks closer than a brother.
MSG	Friends come and friends go, but a true friend sticks by you like family.

8 Study words in the original _language_ they were written in.

Because of the variety of Bible translations, it's important that you learn how to investigate word meaning for yourself. These can be the most rewarding experiences for serious Bible students. One word can be packed with deep significance! Studying words in the original languages they are written in can shed tremendous light on the passage you are studying, and will protect you against misinterpretation.

"A misinterpreted Bible is a misunderstood Bible." – Anonymous

8
» This sheds light on the passage being studied.

» It also protects against misinter-pretation.

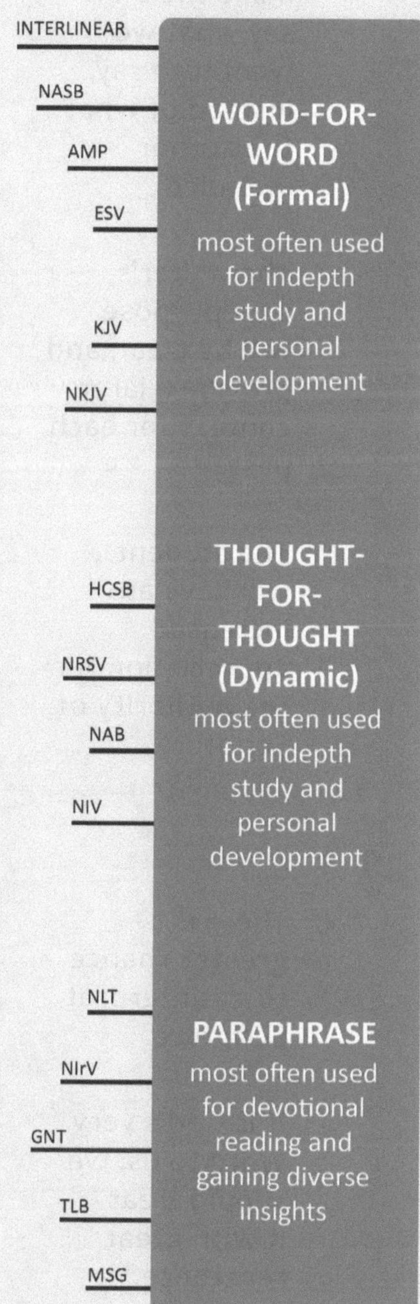

Discussion

1. It clarifies the meaning of words, phrases, sentences, etc.

» It helps guard against taking verses out of context and using them to make the Bible say what we want it to say, instead of what the author intended.

» The writer's true purpose will be clear, and provide a larger context for each passage.

» The student will have an increased appreciation for the authority of Scripture.

2. There is a greater chance to misinterpret Scripture.

» It is God's very Word to us; we should treat it with great reverence.

1 What are some benefits to understanding the cultural and/or historical context when trying to interpret Scripture accurately?

2 Why should students be guarded against studying the Bible haphazardly?

3 What are some benefits to interpreting the Bible literally, verses allegorically?

Activity

1 Connect the question to the external resource a person could use to find the answer:

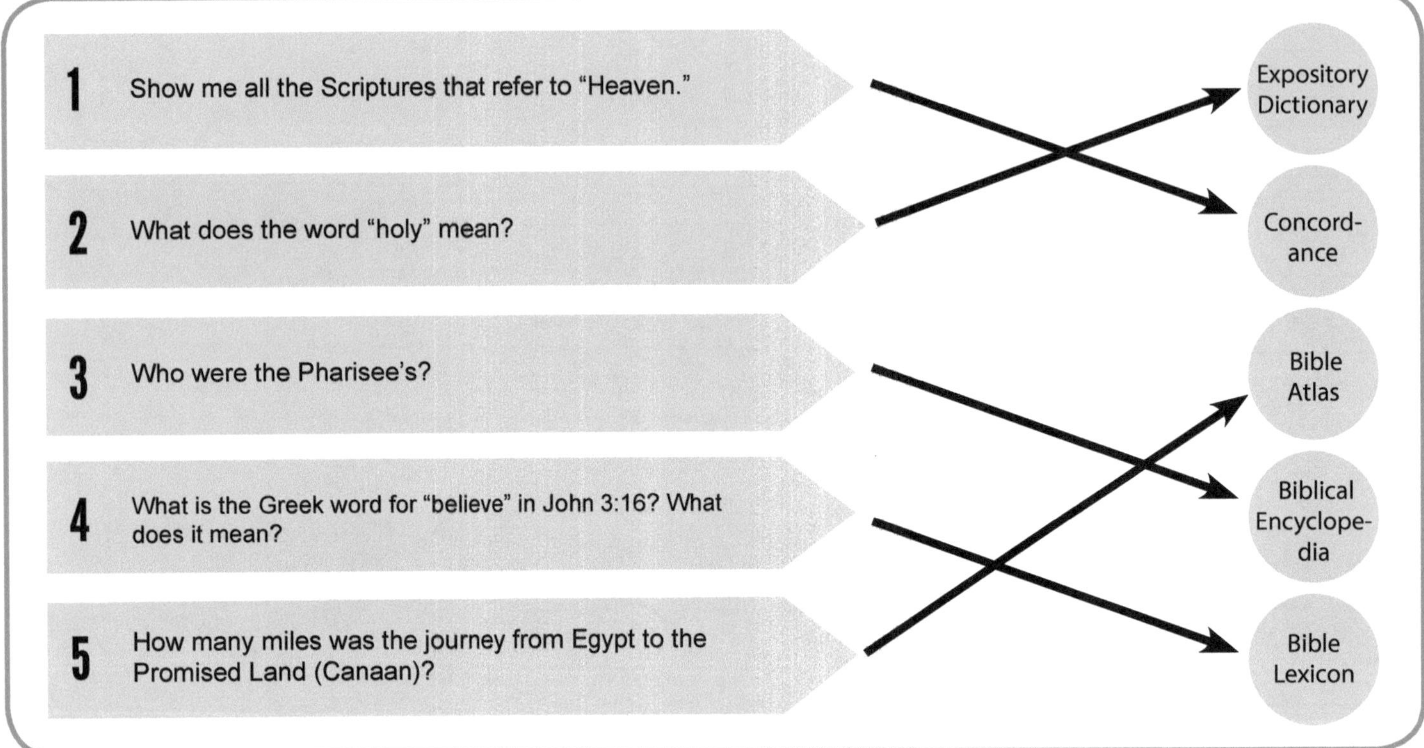

2 Connect the verse to the figure of speech it represents?

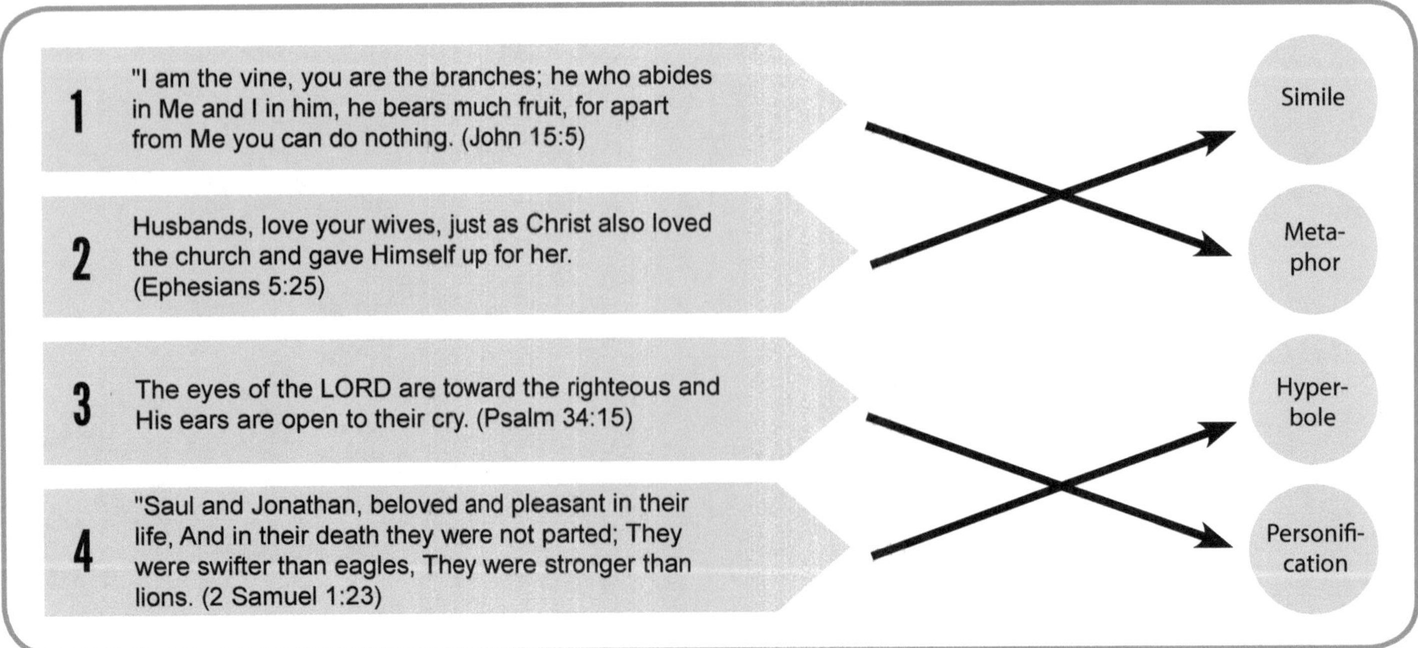

(**3**) Word Study

a. Consider this seemingly repetitive question that Jesus asks of Peter:

"So when they had finished breakfast, Jesus said to Simon Peter, "Simon, son of John, do you love Me more than these?" He said to Him, "Yes, Lord; You know that I love You." He said to him, "Tend My lambs." He said to him again a second time, "Simon, son of John, do you love Me?" He said to Him, "Yes, Lord; You know that I love You." He said to him, "Shepherd My sheep." He said to him the third time, "Simon, son of John, do you love Me?" Peter was grieved because He said to him the third time, "Do you love Me?" And he said to Him, "Lord, You know all things; You know that I love You." Jesus said to him, "Tend My sheep."
– John 21:15–17

b. Use a tool like the Inductive Bible Study App or BlueLetterBible.com to lookup each word translated "love" in the passage above.

c. What did you discover about the conversation from your word study?

____

____

____

____

3,c

» Agape: The love of God.

Phileo: Friendship or brotherly love.

Jesus: Simon… do you love (agape) me more than these?

Peter: Yes, Lord; you know that I love (phileo) you.

Jesus: Simon… do you…love (agape) me?

Peter: Yes, Lord, you know that I love (phileo) you.

Jesus: Simon… do you love (phileo) me?

Peter: [Grieved] "Lord…you know that I love (phileo) you."

4,a

» At first glance, this verse appears to indicate that divorce is acceptable if a man doesn't like his wife any longer.

4 Compare Scripture with Scripture

a. Read Deuteronomy 24:1. At first read, what does this verse seem to be saying?

"When a man takes a wife and marries her, and it happens that she finds no favor in his eyes because he has found some indecency in her, and he writes her a certificate of divorce and puts it in her hand and sends her out from his house."

b. Next, read what Malachi 2:16 and Matthew 19:7–9 say about divorce:

"For I hate divorce," says the LORD, the God of Israel, "and him who covers his garment with wrong," says the LORD of hosts. "So take heed to your spirit, that you do not deal treacherously."
– Malachi 2:16

They said to Him, "Why then did Moses command to GIVE HER A CERTIFICATE OF DIVORCE AND SEND her AWAY?" He said to them, "Because of your hardness of heart Moses permitted you to divorce your wives; but from the beginning it has not been this way. "And I say to you, whoever divorces his wife, except for immorality, and marries another woman commits adultery."
– Matthew 19:7–9

c. How does cross referencing these verses provide clarification to God's intent in Deuteronomy 24:1?

____

____

____

____

____

5 Context is King

When individuals (even believers) are held accountable to the commands of the Bible, a common response is, "The Bible says we shouldn't judge! 'Judge not, lest ye be judged!'" How do we handle such a charge?

a. Read Matthew 7:1.

"Do not judge so that you will not be judged."

b. Now read the verse in its context – Matthew 7:1–5

"Do not judge so that you will not be judged. For in the way you judge, you will be judged; and by your standard of measure, it will be measured to you. Why do you look at the speck that is in your brother's eye, but do not notice the log that is in your own eye? Or how can you say to your brother, 'Let me take the speck out of your eye,' and behold, the log is in your own eye? You hypocrite, first take the

4,c

» God never approved divorce in the Old Testament, but He permitted it because of the stubbornness of the Israelites.

» Remarriage without consideration of the circumstances of divorce could lead one to a life of adultery.

log out of your own eye, and then you will see clearly to take the speck out of your brother's eye."

c. Consider the following cross-reference – Matthew 18:15

"If your brother sins, go and show him his fault in private; if he listens to you, you have won your brother."

d. Taking into consideration the context and the cross-reference, how would you respond to the prohibition to judge?

____

____

____

____

____

____

LESSON *3*

Application: How Do I Respond?

> "Bible study is not complete until we ask ourselves, 'what does this mean for my life, and how can I practically apply it?'"
>
> – John MacArthur

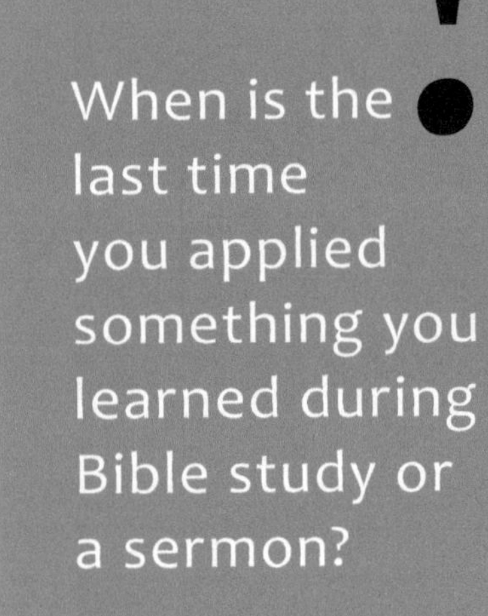

Key Verse

"But one who looks intently at the perfect law, the law of liberty, and abides by it, not having become a forgetful hearer but an effectual doer, this man will be blessed in what he does."

– James 1:25

Discussion Starter

A gray-haired old lady, long a member of her community and church, shook hands with the minister after the service one Sunday morning. "That was a wonderful sermon," she told him, "-- just wonderful. Everything you said applies to someone I know." - *Bits & Pieces, November 1989, p. 19*

Objective

To consider the ramifications of understanding yet ignoring the commands of Scripture and also discover practical ways to create biblically-based goals.

Lesson

Hearing and Obeying God's Word

The relationship between hearing and obeying God's Word is what the third step of Inductive Bible Study—*application*—is all about. It is about choosing to believe the truth you've discovered and allowing that truth to change your thinking and your conduct, and ultimately, your entire life.

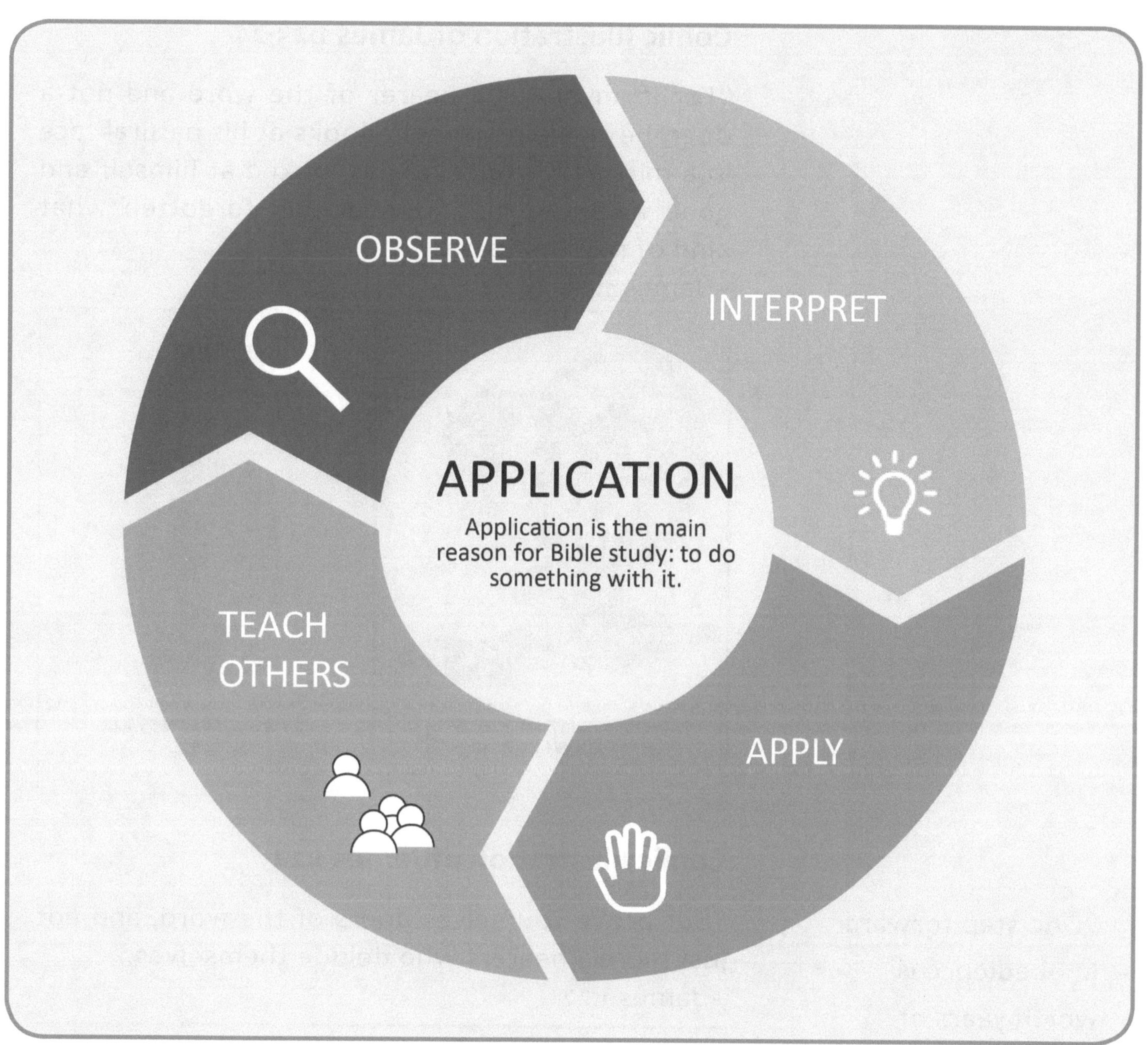

What is Application?

Anyone can read the Bible, and anyone can study it. But only those who are prepared to obey it will be transformed. The purpose of the Word of God is to change people into God's image, to be witnesses for Him to the world.

Application is the step that stimulates this transformation. It is applying what God is teaching by asking, "How do I respond?" It is listening to what God is speaking through His Word, with the intent to obey.

Comic Illustration of James 1:23-24

"For if anyone is a hearer of the word and not a doer, he is like a man who looks at his natural face in a mirror; for once he has looked at himself and gone away, he has immediately forgotten what kind of person he was."
– James 1:23–24

Comic Illustration of James 1:22

"But prove yourselves doers of the word, and not just merely hearers who delude themselves."
– James 1:22

"One step forward in obedience is worth years of study about it."
– Oswald Chambers

Steps to Application

Take application seriously and establish a plan on how to accomplish it. Below are steps on how to do this.

1 As you commit to studying with the intent to obey, *ask questions* to help you apply what you are learning.

Suggested Questions

- What is my plan to carry out these changes and when?

- How does this passage apply to me?

- Is there a commandment of God I have ignored and need to consider?

- Does this passage reflect a particular problem for that day and culture only or is a timeless principle being taught?

2 After asking questions, you should be able to come up with some very clear, personal *action statements*.

Many companies employ the technique of creating SMART goals. In some instances, this methodology can help you define the practical steps you will take toward accomplishing what God is directing you to do.

Specific	Your goal should be as specific as possible and answer the question: What is God directing me to do according to Scripture?	😊	Invite Kim and her family over for dinner and don't bring up our "issue."
		☹️	I will love my neighbors.
Measurable	How will you determine if you are being obedient or not? Measurement will give you specific feedback and allow your accountability partner to hold you accountable.	😊	Even though the latest season of my favorite show was just released on Netflix, I will limit my viewing time to 1 hour per day.
		☹️	I will refrain from worshiping idols.
Attainable	God expects His people to be holy as He is holy, but achieving this is a lifelong process that can only be performed with the power of the Holy Spirit. Goals should push you, but they should also be achievable.	😊	When filing my taxes this year, I will only claim dependents whom I have actually supported per the IRS guidelines.
		☹️	I will never tell another lie again.
Realistic	Is your goal and timeframe realistic? Setting goals that are too lofty will result in disappointment.	😊	Unfriend Mike & Chris from my Facebook account because most of their postings are inappropriate images.
		☹️	Join a monastery / convent to get away from sinners!
Timely	Defining a timeframe or milestones is a great way to ensure that you plan on taking serious steps toward your goal in the near future.	😊	When Jimmy comes home from school, I will sit him down and let him know that I made a mistake when I yelled at him and ask for his forgiveness.
		☹️	Apologize to my son for yelling at him when he's old enough to understand that parents make mistakes.

"He said, 'Take now your son, your only son, whom you love, Isaac, and go to the land of Moriah, and offer him there as a burnt offering on one of the mountains of which I will tell you.' So Abraham rose early in the morning and saddled his donkey, and took two of his young men with him and Isaac his son; and he split wood for the burnt offering, and arose and went to the place of which God had told him."
– Genesis 22:2–3

When Abraham received direction from God to sacrifice his son Isaac, Scripture records that "Abraham rose early in the morning" and took specific steps to perform what God asked him to do; trusting that God would work out the details. What God is asking you to do is much less difficult that sacrificing your son, yet it requires the same level of dedication.

3 These action statements should be *personal, selective* and *specific*.

- **Personal**

  These statements should contain the words "I will," to specify the action that will be taken. "I will forgive my friend for lying to me."

- **Selective**

  You simply won't be able to apply every principle you learn when you study your Bible inductively. Be selective when coming up with your action statements. Ask yourself: "Which of these principles touch on a very real need

in my life?" Then, choose one or maybe two, and ask God how you should respond. Be careful to not ignore the others, or the ones you want to avoid. Sometimes those are the ones you should tackle first!

- **Specific**

  Your action statement should also be precise and specific. An action statement that says, "I will respond with respect to my boss who was demeaning," is much more specific than, "I will be respectful."

4. Never forget that the ultimate goal of Bible study, whether inductive or otherwise, is to _**know God**_ and His Son so that you might have life in Him.

Focusing too much on the Scriptures at the expense of the One the Scriptures were written about is dangerous.

"This is eternal life, that they may know You, the only true God, and Jesus Christ whom You have sent."
– John 17:3

5. Sometimes as you are observing, interpreting and applying a passage it will be clear God is moving you to deal with some _unconfessed sin_.

If this occurs, humbly bow before God and ask Him to forgive you for whatever it is He has revealed. Also, ask God if there are steps that He would like you to take either avoid making the same mistake again. During this time, God may also provide guidance on how to mend relationships that have been damaged due to sin.

6 Other times, you may be moved to respond in _faith_, lived out through _obedience_.

When this occurs, don't be afraid to step out and do what God is asking you to do! You will be blessed. Combine faith with what you read and hear. Genuine faith obeys.

Suppose you are reading the following verse:

"Now the LORD said to Abram, 'Go forth from your country, And from your relatives And from your father's house, To the land which I will show you...'"
– Genesis 12:1

Just because you are growing tired of living in your current city (and near relatives), this does not automatically mean that God is directing you to pack your bags and hit the road! Don't simply substitute Abram's name with yours and believe that you have reached the appropriate application. God may want you to show your faith in Him by staying in your current situation.

7 Get an _accountability_ partner to hold you accountable.

Who NOT to select as an accountability partner:

- Someone that is spiritually immature.

- Someone who is not attempting to grow spiritually themselves.

- Someone who is known for gossiping.

- Someone that you cannot trust.

- Someone who may be afraid to call you out on various matters.

8 Take time to _journal_ what God is saying to you. Don't just view reading as a fact or ritual.

Find a notebook that works for you, either a simple spiral notebook or a nicer journal. Also, there are many apps that allow you to journal your thoughts in a safe and secure environment that you can easily take with you wherever you go. Your notebook will be the place where you will take notes on things the Lord is teaching you or things you want to remember.

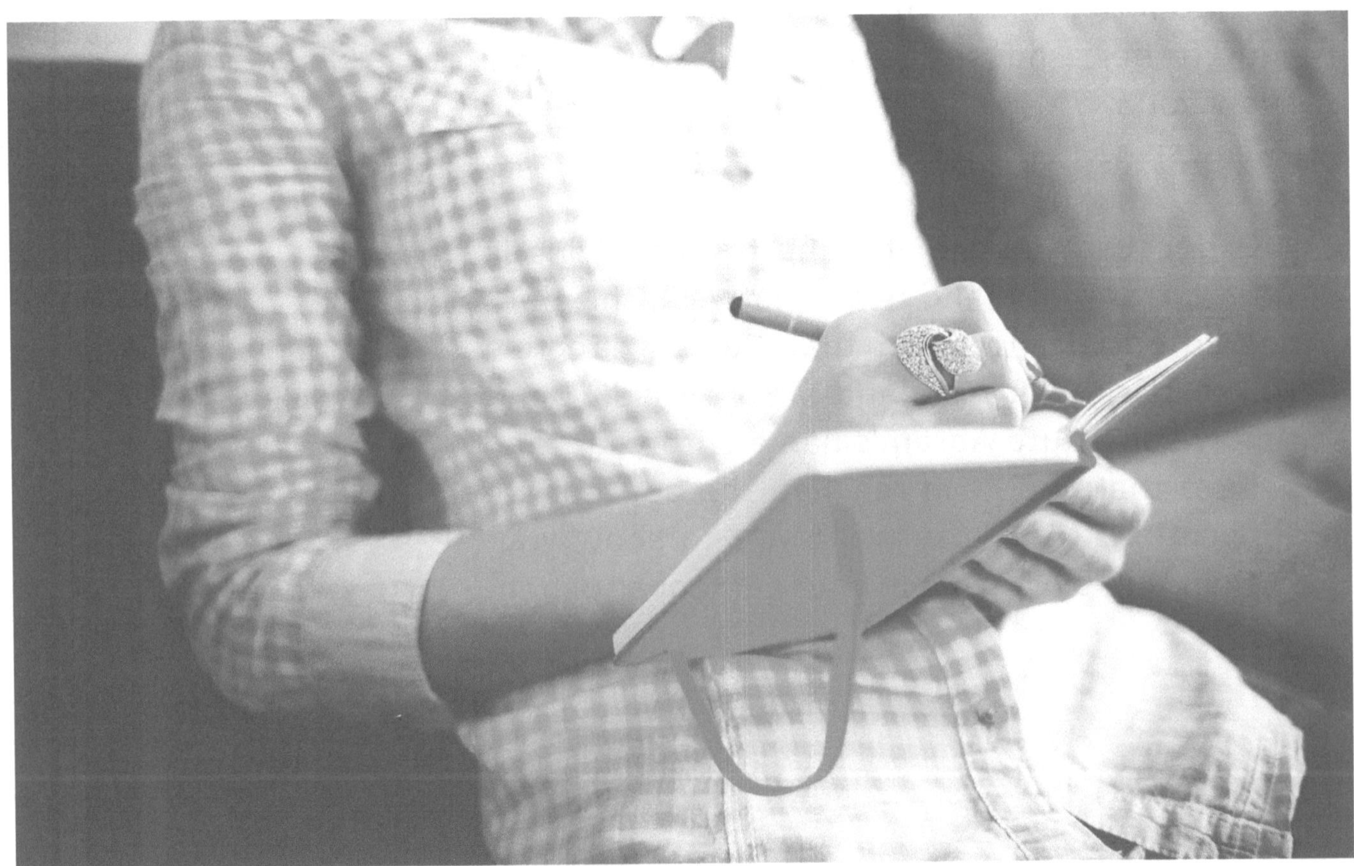

Discussion

1 Read Ezekiel 33:31.

"Son of man, your people talk about you in their houses and whisper about you at the doors. They say to each other, 'Come on, let's go hear the prophet tell us what the LORD is saying!' So my people come pretending to be sincere and sit before you. They listen to your words, but they have no intention of doing what you say. Their mouths are full of lustful words, and their hearts seek only after money. You are very entertaining to them, like someone who sings love songs with a beautiful voice or plays fine music on an instrument. They hear what you say, but they don't act on it!"
– Ezekiel 33:30–32 NLT[3]

How often does this verse ring true for you? How often do you read the Word of God with no intention of obeying it?

____

____

____

____

____

1

» In Ezekiel 33, God begins to reprimand the Israelite captives that have been exiled to Babylon. They would go to hear the prophet Ezekiel speak with no intention to obey. Unfortunately, the same can be said of some church goers and Bible students today. Many people attend church only because they love to hear a particular preacher. Church is then lessened to nothing more than an entertainment venue.

---

2 Why would it be beneficial to create action statements that begin with the words "I will"?

____

____

____

____

____

____

2

» It specifies the action taken.

» It makes the action very personal.

» It is almost a challenge to yourself!

3 Discuss the relevance of God's Word to your life in light of what you have learned about application. According to God's Word, are some truths not relevant? Why or why not?

____

____

____

____

____

____

____

3

» The question should be, am I ready and willing to believe this truth and apply it in my life?

» God's Word is always relevant and applicable.

4 Discuss the following quote: *"God's Word will not always be 'pain free,' but it will always be profitable."* Do you agree or disagree?

____

____

____

____

____

____

____

____

4

» We won't always comprehend the extent of the "return on investment" until we enter heaven!

» God is about transformation; His Word was created to change people to be more like Him. Therefore, even the hard stuff is profitable.

» "All Scripture is inspired by God and profitable for teaching, for reproof, for correction, for training in righteousness."
– 2 Timothy 3:16

Activity

1 Action Statement

Read Romans 5:3–5:

"And not only this, but we also exult in our tribulations, knowing that tribulation brings about perseverance; and perseverance, proven character; and proven character, hope; and hope does not disappoint, because the love of God has been poured out within our hearts through the Holy Spirit who was given to us."

After asking questions about the verse, a person could come up with the following applications to the truths they have learned. Let's say this person is either in a difficult job, or was just let go from a job. Respond to each attempt at an action statement, noting whether they are strong based on whether they are personal, selective and specific:

a. I will rejoice in my job loss because God is working something good out of it.

☑ **Personal**

☑ **Selective**

☑ **Specific**

1,a

» This answer is very personal. There is a personal and emotional commitment to remain joyful.

b. I will memorize a verse from the Bible.

- ☑ Personal
- ☑ Selective
- ☐ Specific

c. I will ask a trusted friend to walk through this with me to help keep focused on the promises of God rather than my situation.

- ☑ Personal
- ☑ Selective
- ☑ Specific

d. I will be nice to my boss.

- ☑ Personal
- ☑ Selective
- ☐ Specific

1,b

» This response is not specific! It would be better to pick a specific verse to memorize: "I will memorize Philippians 4:13."

1,c

» This response is personal, specific and therefore, effective.

1,d

» This response doesn't have an application point to it. A better response would be, "I will respond to my boss who was demeaning with respect."

Read each passage and determine which of the S.M.A.R.T. criteria has been met by the stated goal. Afterwards, update the goal with a suggested revision to meet all of the S.M.A.R.T. criteria.

a. James 1:19–20

Passage	This you know, my beloved brethren. But everyone must be quick to hear, slow to speak and slow to anger; for the anger of man does not achieve the righteousness of God.
Goal	I will do a better job of controlling my temper.
Review	☐ Specific ☐ Measureable ☑ Attainable ☑ Realistic ☐ Timely
Suggested Revision to Goal	Starting Monday morning, I will refrain from yelling and using profanity while at work. When I am upset, I will take 3 deep breaths and calmly state my objection in a pleasant tone. If I make a mistake, I will take the following steps by the close of the next business day. 1. Pray and ask God's forgiveness for my mistake. 2. Contact my accountability partner discuss my mistake. 3. Apologize to my coworkers for speaking to them inappropriately.

b. Matthew 6:28–33

Passage	"And why are you worried about clothing? Observe how the lilies of the field grow; they do not toil nor do they spin, yet I say to you that not even Solomon in all his glory clothed himself like one of these. But if God so clothes the grass of the field, which is alive today and tomorrow is thrown into the furnace, will He not much more clothe you? You of little faith! Do not worry then, saying, 'What will we eat?' or 'What will we drink?' or 'What will we wear for clothing?' For the Gentiles eagerly seek all these things; for your heavenly Father knows that you need all these things. But seek first His kingdom and His righteousness, and all these things will be added to you."
Goal	I'm never going to buy another pair of shoes again for the rest of my life!
Review	☑ Specific ☐ Realistic ☑ Measureable ☑ Timely ☐ Attainable
Suggested Revision to Goal	*Because God has provided me with ample supply of clothing, starting this weekend, I will start to donate clothes I have not worn in the past two years to the Salvation Army. Afterwards, whenever I buy a new item, I will give away an item in order to bless someone else.*

c. Exodus 20:17

Passage	"You shall not covet your neighbor's house; you shall not covet your neighbor's wife or his male servant or his female servant or his ox or his donkey or anything that belongs to your neighbor."
Goal	I won't buy anything for Christmas!
Review	☑ Specific ☑ Measureable ☑ Attainable ☐ Realistic ☑ Timely
Suggested Revision to Goal	*I will not take out a loan this Christmas in order to get my child things that I cannot afford in order for them to have the same things as their friends (or impress our neighbors).*

3 Select one of the following passages and complete the S.M.A.R.T. Goal Worksheet. Remember to take time to observe and interpret the passage prior to considering ways to apply it to your life.

Category	Passage
Impatient	Psalm 27
Doubtful	Proverbs 3:5–8
Married	Ephesians 5:21–33
Youth	Ephesians 6:1–3
Parents	Deuteronomy 11:18–21
Employed	Ephesians 6:5–8
Supervisors	Ephesians 6:9

Selected Passage	
Observation Notes	
Interpretation Notes	
Application Notes	
Goal	
Specific ☐	
Measureable ☐	
Attainable ☐	
Realistic ☐	
Timely ☐	

A free PDF version of this worksheet can be found at
http://ibible.study/workbook.

Memorization & Mediation: Thy Word is in My Heart?

> "When a verse pops into the mind when teaching, preaching, studying or pondering a decision of some sort—it is not your memory that is bringing that text to your mind, but it is the prompting of the Holy Spirit that is doing it."
>
> – John Butler, *Bible Expositor*

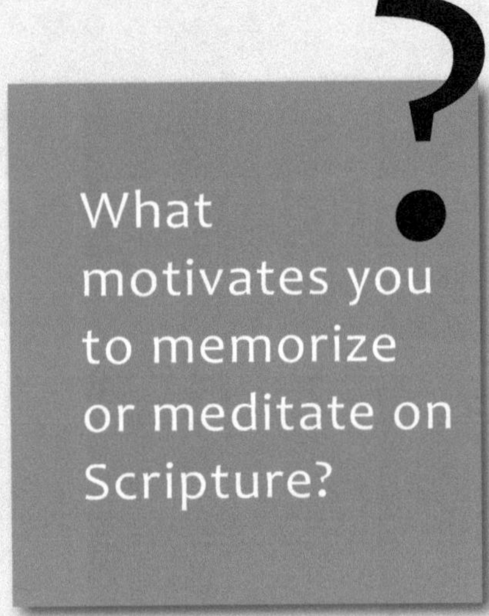

Key Verse

"This book of the law shall not depart from your mouth, but you shall meditate on it day and night, so that you may be careful to do according to all that is written in it; for then you will make your way prosperous, and then you will have success."

– Joshua 1:8

Discussion Starter

Toward the close of World War II, allied forces were mopping up against remaining Nazi resistance. One particular unit was assigned a crucial mission in Berlin. Each soldier had to memorize a map detailing all of Berlin's important military sites—and they had to do it in a single night! In just a few hours, each soldier in the unit had committed the map to memory. The mission was a success. Several years later, the Army conducted an experiment to see if that original feat could be duplicated. They offered a similar unit an extra week's furlough—an attractive incentive—if they could carry out a comparable mission without a hitch. But the second unit could not match the success of the first. What made the difference? The lives of the men were not at stake. Surviving in battle was a greater motivation than a week's vacation.

Objective

To reflect upon the importance of saturating our hearts and minds with the Word of God and learn tools and techniques which will help build biblical memory.

Memorizing and Meditating on Scripture

Certain disciplines within the life of the believer will enhance their study of the Scriptures and help them experience this "sweetness." Two of these disciplines include memorization and meditation. Though not one of the three steps to Inductive Bible Study, they are vital to the personal life of the disciple of Christ.

Scripture Memorization

In order for the Holy Spirit to quicken someone's memory, they must have previously filled their minds with Scripture.

1 At first, memorizing Scripture will be *hard work*.

At first, memorizing Scripture will feel like work, and it will take perseverance. However, once you taste the "sweetness" of the Word, a whole new world will open up. Many people who memorize Scripture speak of seeing things differently, and experiencing a joy previously unknown.

The unfolding of Your words gives light; It gives understanding to the simple. I opened my mouth wide and panted, For I longed for Your commandments.
– Psalm 119:130–131

1

» An acute awareness will replace boredom. Words/phrases that previously were confusing will make sense and bring understanding to your mind and heart.

» Messages from pastors and Bible teachers will become clear.

(**2**) Christians should memorize Scripture because:

a. God _commands_ it.

"Let the word of Christ richly dwell within you."
– Colossians 3:16

"Therefore, impress these words of mine on your heart and on your soul."
– Deuteronomy 11:18

b. Jesus _modeled_ it.

While being tempted by the devil, Jesus recites Scripture that He had committed to memory.

But He answered and said, "It is written, 'MAN SHALL NOT LIVE ON BREAD ALONE, BUT ON EVERY WORD THAT PROCEEDS OUT OF THE MOUTH OF GOD.'"
– Matthew 4:4 *(Jesus quotes Deuteronomy 8:3)*

Jesus said to him, "On the other hand, it is written, 'YOU SHALL NOT PUT THE LORD YOUR GOD TO THE TEST.'"
– Matthew 4:7 *(Jesus quotes Deuteronomy 6:16)*

Then Jesus said to him, "Go, Satan! For it is written, 'YOU SHALL WORSHIP THE LORD YOUR GOD, AND SERVE HIM ONLY.'"
– Matthew 4:10 *(Jesus quotes Deuteronomy 6:13)*

After quoting these verses, Matthew 4:11 says, "Then the devil left Him." What's your defense when being tempted by the devil? How's it working for you?

Leader Insight

When Jesus experienced temptation, He didn't protect Himself with His divine power. Instead, He used the same tool that is available to every believer—the Scriptures! Note: He didn't pull out a scroll and turn to a passage. Instead, He was armed with "the sword of the Spirit, which is the word of God" (Eph. 6:16).

c. It will _renew_ your mind and _transform_ your life.

"And do not be conformed to this world, but be transformed by the renewing of your mind, so that you may prove what the will of God is, that which is good and acceptable and perfect."
– Romans 12:2

d. It will develop godly _wisdom_.

The Lord gives it: "For the LORD gives wisdom; from His mouth come knowledge and understanding."
– Proverbs 2:6

e. It will _mature_ you as a believer.

"I gave you milk to drink, not solid food; for you were not yet able to receive it. Indeed, even now you are not yet able."
– 1 Corinthians 3:2

f. It will help you communicate the _Gospel_ to unbelievers.

"For I delivered to you as of first importance what I also received, that Christ died for our sins according to the Scriptures, and that He was buried, and that He was raised on the third day according to the Scriptures, and that He appeared to Cephas, then to the twelve."
– 1 Corinthians 15:3–5

g. It will give you the single most effective _weapon_ to combat sin and temptation.

"The law of his God is in his heart; his steps do not slip."
– Psalm 37:31

3 There are many simple techniques that will help you in your commitment to memorize Scripture.

a. Stick to one _translation_.

Even though there is no "right" translation, we suggest you use one of the "Word for Word" translations that we reference in the chart in Chapter 2 – Interpretation.

b. Memorize the _"address"_ together with the verse.

It will be important to know where the verse can be found. That way you will be able to tell others where to find it and you will know where it fits within the canon of Scripture.

c. Keep all memorized verses _fresh_.

Don't memorize it for the moment, without being able to recite it from memory one week, one month or one year later. Take time each week and review all of the verses you've memorized or all of the verses related to a particular topic (e.g. salvation, sin, mercy, etc.).

d. Pick a *different* word or phrase to focus on each day as you memorize.

Repeat the verse five or ten times out loud, emphasizing one word or phrase. Then move on to the next word and do the same.

Leader Insight

For example, let's look at Deuteronomy 6:13:

Round 1: "You shall ***fear only the LORD*** your God; and you shall worship Him and swear by His name."

Round 2: "You shall fear only the LORD your God; and you shall ***worship Him*** and swear by His name."

Round 3: "You shall fear *only the LORD your God*; and you shall worship Him and ***swear by His name*.""

Continue doing this through the end of the verse.

e. Use *Bible apps* or write verses on *index cards*.

Here are a few apps (most are free). Each of them has various activities—such as erasing a word—to help students memorize verses.

- Scripture Typer

- Bible Minded

- Fighter Verses

- Remember Me

f. _Visualize_ and internalize the words.

Read the verse below. Then close your eyes and picture a deer running through the fields in search of water. Once he finds a flowing brook, consider the sound of him panting for water.

"As the deer pants for the water brooks, So my soul pants for You, O God."
– Psalm 42:1

Internalization is the process of seeing yourself acting out the passage. Think back to a time when you were extremely thirsty after working in the yard on a hot summer day. Consider how refreshed you felt after drinking a nice cool glass of water. Now think of how the Psalmist pants after God when the world has exhausted him. Consider how he searches desperately for God and finds total replenishment.

g. Have friends commit to keep you _accountable_.

Solicit a friend or family member who will commit to keeping you accountable with what you are memorizing. You may even encourage them to memorize the same passage with you.

Scripture Meditation

Biblical meditation is different from worldly meditation taught by false religions. It is never a "state" that you arrive at, nor is it a "detaching" of your mind. On the contrary, biblical meditation focuses on filling the mind and heart with more and more of one particular subject: the Word of God.

1 The English word *"meditate"* comes from the Hebrew word meaning, "to moan, mutter, ponder, imagine, or utter."

2 Meditating on God's Word, then, means *thinking* about or *speaking* a word, verse, or whole passage over and over.

"These words, which I am commanding you today, shall be in your heart."
– Deuteronomy 6:6

3 Ultimately, the objective of both memorizing Scripture and then meditating on it will be to hear God's *voice*.

Discussion

1

» I have a bad memory

» No time

» Too old

» Tried and just can't do it

» I'm not a pastor/ leader; why do I need to?

2

» Will be blessed

» Like a tree firmly planted by streams of water (strong, healthy, constant "water" source)

» Will yield fruit (disciples, fruit of the Spirit)

» Will not wither (motivation to keep going)

» Will prosper in what he does

1 What are some roadblocks to memorizing Scripture (perceived or true)?

____

____

____

____

____

2 Read the following verses:

"How blessed is the man who does not walk in the counsel of the wicked,

Nor stand in the path of sinners,

Nor sit in the seat of scoffers!

But his delight is in the law of the Lord,

And in His law he meditates day and night.

He will be like a tree firmly planted by streams of water,

Which yields its fruit in its season

And its leaf does not wither;

And in whatever he does, he prospers."
– Psalm 1:1–3

What does God promise to those who commit to meditating on God's Word?

3 What are some improper motives to memorize Scripture?

4 What are some verses you memorized as a child that have stuck with you? How did they remain over the years? How have they blessed your life?

____

____

____

____

____

____

____

Activity

1 Scripture Memorization:

Suggested Verse:

Beloved, let us love one another, for love is from God; and everyone who loves is born of God and knows God.
– 1 John 4:7

One fun way to memorize Scripture is called "erase a word."

a) Write 1 John 4:7 (or any verse you desire to memorize) an index card. We recommend using a pencil and writing lightly for easy erase.

b) Read that verse 3–4 times.

c) Scribble out or erase a word, and say the verse again.

d) Scribble out or erase another word, and say the verse again.

e) Continue this process until all words are erased.

f) Say the verse from memory 2–3 more times!

If you don't have an index card, one of the apps mentioned earlier in this chapter will allow you to do the same.

(**2**) Scripture Meditation

Suggested Verse:

"O LORD my God, I cried to You for help, and You healed me."
– Psalm 30:2

a. Select a verse to meditate on.

Choose whichever verse God lays on your heart. We recommend it being a verse that has personal meaning or relevance to you. A list of names from the first eight chapters of 1 Chronicles won't be of much use to you.

Which verse did you select to meditate on?

____

____

b. Memorize the selected verse.

Even though you can read a verse while meditating, a memorized verse works better.

c. Block out some time.

Start with five minutes and work your way up.

How much time will you spend meditating?

____

____

d. Choose a quiet place.

   Don't try to meditate on Scripture in traffic or at the gym.

   Where will you meditate?

____

____

e. Focus on God's presence.

   These are His words, so imagine Him speaking them softly into your ears.

f. Begin to repeatedly rehearse the verse in your mind or aloud softly.

   If the place you have chosen has visual distractions, we recommend closing your eyes at this point.

LESSON 5

Prayer: Talking to God?

Key Verse

"But Hannah replied, 'No, my lord, I am a woman oppressed in spirit; I have drunk neither wine nor strong drink, but I have poured out my soul before the Lord.'"
– 1 Samuel 1:15

Discussion Starter

A tale is told about a small town that had historically been "dry," but then a local businessman decided to build a tavern. A group of Christians from a local church were concerned and planned an all-night prayer meeting to ask God to intervene. It just so happened that shortly thereafter lightning struck the bar and it burned to the ground. The owner of the bar sued the church, claiming that the prayers of the congregation were responsible, but the church hired a lawyer to argue in court that they were not responsible. The presiding judge, after his initial review of the case, stated, "No matter how this case comes out, one thing is clear. The tavern owner believes in prayer and the Christians do not." - *J.K. Johnston, Why Christians Sin, Discovery House, 1992, p. 129*

Objective

To learn a working definition of prayer and outline how essential prayer is to an enriching Bible study experience.

Lesson

What Exactly is Prayer?

Some like to toss around the phrase, "Prayer changes things." While prayer does play a part in changing things, it is important to understand what prayer is and what it isn't.

1 Prayer is a _conversation_ with God.

As believers, we have the awesome privilege to speak with the creator and sustainer of the universe any time we so desire. While our friends and family may occasionally grow weary of hearing our daily ups and downs, God begs you to "cast all you anxiety on Him, because He cares for you" (1 Pet. 5:7). Prayer may take on various mode and frequencies, but at its core, it's simply a conversation with God.

2 Prayer is more than the submission of your _wish-list_.

It is true that "every good thing given and every perfect gift comes from above" (James 1:17). God offers so much more than what some make Him out to be—a cosmic genie. Prayer is not a game, demanding answers like playing with a Magic 8 ball. It is also not telling God what to do. Prayer is a genuine conversation with God consisting of adoration (praise), confession, thanksgiving, and supplication (requests).

James, a disciple and the half-brother of Jesus wrote: "Yet you do not know what your life will be like tomorrow. You are just a vapor that appears for a little while and then vanishes away. Instead, you ought to say, 'If the Lord wills, we will live and also do this or that.'" (James 4:14–15)

1

» Mode:

- Oral

- Mental

- Casual

- Formal

» Frequency:

- Occasional

- Constant

- Irregular

2

» _If the Lord wills. Prayer changes things, when it agrees with God's will. And in order to know what His will is, we need to study His Word!_

> » Regular Bible study and prayer keeps us aligned with God's purposes, plan and will.

3 Prayer is seeking God's _will_ through His Word.

The effectiveness of your prayer life is directly related to your study and understanding of God's Word. If you feel that your prayers are consistently being ignored or unanswered, it is important to investigate how your petitions align with God's Word. As a result of studying the Bible, we find out God's will. Isn't it interesting, that even our Lord begins the model prayer with "Your kingdom come, Your will be done, On earth as it is in heaven" (Matthew 6:10)?

The Relationship Between Prayer and Bible Study

A relationship with Jesus is developed through spending time in Bible study and prayer. God speaks through study of His Word, but He also speaks through prayer. And, prayer gives people the opportunity to speak to Him.

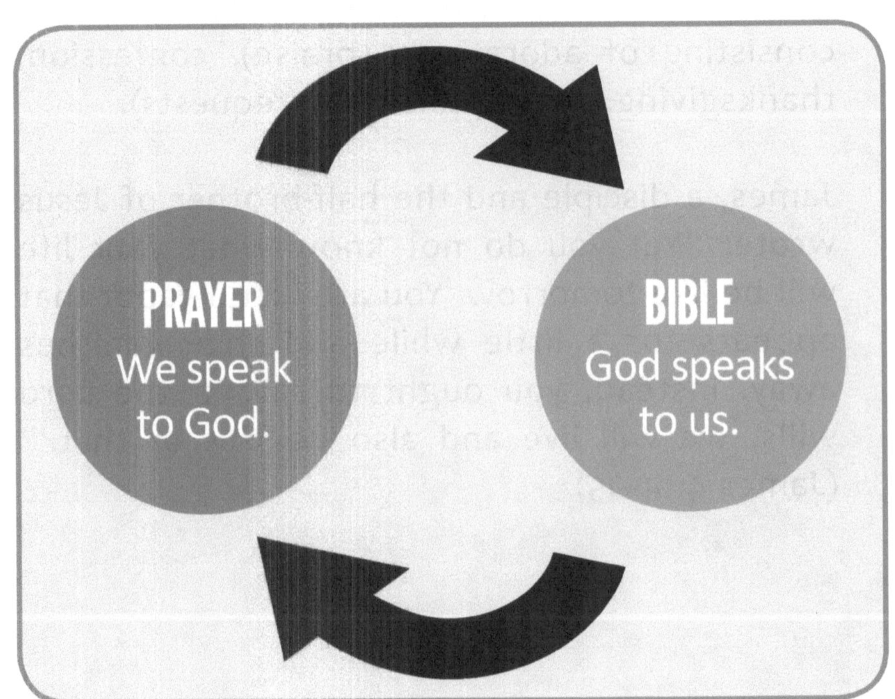

Leader Insight

God can and has used various methods to speak to mankind over the years—prophets (Heb. 1:1), animals (Num. 22:28), and nature (Rom. 1:20), for example. But, His primary method of speaking to mankind now is through His Word. Hebrews 1:1–2 highlights the transition of God's means of communicating to mankind through His Son. God may sometimes speak audibly to people, although it is highly doubtful that this occurs as often as some claim He does. God can also get His point across through events, circumstances and consequences. The only true test of whether or not something is authentically from God is to compare it to the Bible—God's Word.

God, after He spoke long ago to the fathers in the prophets in many portions and in many ways, in these last days has spoken to us in His Son, whom He appointed heir of all things, through whom also He made the world.
– Hebrews 1:1–2

1 Prayer before Bible study *settles* our hearts and minds so that we are ready to *hear* from God.

Society has defined our current age the "information" or "digital" age. While the ability to share information through electronic devices has proven to advance our economy and civilization, this has also brought on a perpetual appetite for more data. During our intimate time with God, prayer enables us to unplug our hearts and minds from the cares of the world in order to tune in to what God has to say.

"Call to Me and I will answer you, and I will tell you great and mighty things, which you do not know."
– Jeremiah 33:3

If your tendency has been to fall asleep when attempting to study, don't worry! Many have fought this battle and won. When Jesus taught the apostles the high standard of forgiveness, their first request was "Lord, 'Increase our faith" (Luke 17:5)! Likewise, feel free to begin your study time with a prayer asking God to do the following:

- Increase your passion for His Word.

- Increase your alertness.

- Help you understand His Word better.

- Soften your heart to be willing and eager to apply what He teaches you.

Leader Insight

2 God reveals the _mysteries_ hidden in the Scriptures to Christians, by the _Spirit_.

The words of the Bible are so unique in that it takes the Spirit of God in the life of the believer in order to understand and accept them. In Paul's letter to Corinth, he refers to God's wisdom as a "mystery," in that it is hidden to the natural man, yet revealed to the believer.

"For to us God revealed them through the Spirit; for the Spirit searches all things, even the depths of God. For who among men knows the thoughts of a man except the spirit of the man which is in him? Even so the thoughts of God no one knows except the Spirit of God. Now we have received, not the spirit of the world, but the Spirit who is from God, so that we may know the things freely given to us by God, which things we also speak, not in words taught by human wisdom, but in those taught by the Spirit, combining spiritual thoughts with spiritual words. But a natural man does not accept the things of the Spirit of God, for they are foolishness to him; and he cannot understand them, because they are spiritually appraised."
– 1 Corinthians 2:10–14

3 Prayer helps us stay _actively_ connected with the Spirit while we study.

Don't leave prayer at the door when studying the Bible. Prayer is what transitions Bible study from a monologue to a dialogue between you and God. Instead of rushing through the reading of the Bible in order to stay on track with a Bible-in-a-Year program, take breaks to ask the Author to speak to your life directly.

3

4 After studying the Word, prayer invites the Spirit to _direct_ us in how to respond to what we learned in the Scriptures.

Since we don't have the capability to understand God's Word without the Holy Spirit teaching us, it stands to reason that we won't apply it correctly without His divine guidance. Have you ever trusted your own understanding and made a situation worse? God is waiting for us to turn to Him and humbly ask "now I need you to show me how to live out your Word."

"The mind of man plans his way, But the Lord directs his steps."
– Proverbs 16:9

"If he gives you the grace to make you believe, he will give you the grace to live a holy life afterward."
– Charles Spurgeon

5 <u>*Tracking*</u> what prayers God has answered increases faith and a thirst to know God more, and therefore study more!

Nothing has been more proven to increase faith than the evidence of what God has done in the past. The Bible is a factual document containing the mighty works of God in the past. It is the basis of all that Christians know and believe about God. Tracking your prayers allows you to keep a personal log of the mercies of God that you have experienced. There's nothing wrong with the faith that comes from studying about how God delivered Daniel from the lion's den, but it's much more powerful to review the accounts of how God has done the same for you!

Leader Insight

Suggest that students keep a prayer journal or even track their prayers in a spreadsheet. There are a number of apps that do a great job of facilitating this. Echo (https://new.echoprayer.com/) is a free prayer manager that is available on Google Play and the App Store.

Discussion

1 Since God knows everything about you and what you are going ask before you even ask it, what might be some reasons God still wants you to pray to Him?

2 How are prayers sometimes used (or abused) to accomplish things other than communicating with God?

3

» We become more attune to what the Spirit is saying/leading.

» Our hearts will seek God and what He wants us to learn, not what we want to learn.

4

» Our prayers would shift more toward what His Word says— what He wants for us.

3 What are the benefits of inviting God into your study of His Word?

4 How might your prayers change if instead of asking God to give you what you desire, you ask Him to create in you the desire of *His* heart?

Activity

"And two blind men sitting by the road, hearing that Jesus was passing by, cried out, 'Lord, have mercy on us, Son of David!' The crowd sternly told them to be quiet, but they cried out all the more, 'Lord, Son of David, have mercy on us!' And Jesus stopped and called them, and said, 'What do you want Me to do for you?' They said to Him, 'Lord, we want our eyes to be opened.' Moved with compassion, Jesus touched their eyes; and immediately they regained their sight and followed Him." – Matthew 20:30–34

God is moved with the same level of compassion regarding our requests of Him. The assignment for this lesson is to simply make your requests known to God.

1 Using the journal below, write down the specific things that you are asking God for.

2 Search Scripture to find alignment with God's will.

   a. Find out if there is a corresponding promise of God.

   b. Validate that your request does not go against the will of God.

3 Patiently wait for God's response to your request.

4 Journal ways that you see God at work in response to your prayer.

5 Praise God as you see Him answer your prayers!

6 Share the good news of what God has done in your life.

PRAYER JOURNAL

DATE: ___________________

Scripture Meditation
What have you been studying lately in God's Word?

Adoration
What are some reasons God is so amazing to you?

Confession
What has the Holy Spirit begun to convict you about?

Thanksgiving
Celebrate what God is doing in your life! Don't forget about the little things you might take for granted.

Supplication
What do you want God to do for you or others (intercession)?

Inductive Bible Study
Stop reading. start studying!

PRAYER JOURNAL

DATE: _______________

Scripture Meditation

What have you been studying lately in God's Word?

Adoration

What are some reasons God is so amazing to you?

Confession

What has the Holy Spirit begun to convict you about?

Thanksgiving

Celebrate what God is doing in your life! Don't forget about the little things you might take for granted.

Supplication

What do you want God to do for you or others (intercession)?

PRAYER SUPPLICATION (REQUEST) LOG

Date of Request	
Specific Request	
Scriptural Alignement	
Ways I See God at Work	
Date Answered	

PRAYER SUPPLICATION (REQUEST) LOG

Date of Request	
Specific Request	
Scriptural Alignement	
Ways I See God at Work	
Date Answered	

ADDITIONAL RESOURCES

Inductive Bible Study App

Do you love the Inductive Bible Study method and wish you could do it wherever you go? Introducing the Inductive Bible Study App (InductiveBibleStudyApp. com). This one-of-a-kind app empowers individuals to grow in their faith by enabling them to study the Bible inductively using their favorite mobile or tablet device.

With this app, you can:

- **Mark Keywords** - Use images, and highlight, bold or italicize text (and more) for easy visual reference.

- **Take Notes** - Journal your personal study of the Scriptures and reflect on your growth.

- **Apply Themes** - Specify the theme of each chapter and even group verses together with division themes.

- **Perform Word Studies** - Understand the words of the Bible in their original language via the built-in Strong's concordance.

- **Research Cross-references** - Discover every instance that a word is used in the Bible to gain a comprehensive understanding of it.

Download the #1 Free Inductive Bible Study App today!

InductiveBibleStudyApp.com

Selected Passage	
Observation Notes	
Interpretation Notes	
Application Notes	
Goal Specific ☐ Measureable ☐ Attainable ☐ Realistic ☐ Timely ☐	

A free PDF version of this worksheet can be found at
http://ibible.study/workbook.

PRAYER JOURNAL

DATE: _______________

Scripture Meditation

What have you been studying lately in God's Word?

Adoration

What are some reasons God is so amazing to you?

Confession

What has the Holy Spirit begun to convict you about?

Thanksgiving

Celebrate what God is doing in your life! Don't forget about the little things you might take for granted.

Supplication

What do you want God to do for you or others (intercession)?

PRAYER SUPPLICATION (REQUEST) LOG

Date of Request	
Specific Request	
Scriptural Alignement	
Ways I See God at Work	
Date Answered	

A free PDF version of this worksheet can be found at http://ibible.study/workbook.

About Author

Henry Jackson III, a bondservant of Jesus Christ. He is a native of Memphis, TN, who now calls Atlanta, GA his home. Henry primarily utilizes his spiritual gifts of teaching and leadership at Elizabeth Baptist Church in Atlanta, GA, where he currently serves as the Middle School Youth Pastor. Henry enjoys spending time with his darling wife Vanessa and son Henry IV, kayaking, racquetball, and mountain-bike riding.

Henry is the founder of Inductive Bible Study LLC, an organization that empowers individuals to grow in their faith by enabling them to study the Bible inductively using their favorite mobile device. Find out more at InductiveBibleStudyApp.com.

As a Myasthenia Gravis (MG) survivor, Henry is a living testimony of God's healing power. Each day that God gives him the strength, he is constantly pursuing ways to glorify God and to make Him known to the world. A portion of the proceeds from the sale of this book will be donated to the Myasthenia Gravis Foundation of America, Inc. Find out more at www.myasthenia.org.

Made in United States
Troutdale, OR
03/06/2025